P9-CEK-281

Symphonie Fantastique
(Episode in the Life of an Artist)

Op. 14

Hector Berlioz

DOVER PUBLICATIONS, INC.
Mineola, New York

Published in Canada by General Publishing Company, Ltd., 30 Lesmill Road, Don Mills, Toronto, Ontario.

Published in the United Kingdom by Constable and Company, Ltd., 3 The Lanchesters, 162–164 Fulham Palace Road, London W6 9ER.

Bibliographical Note

This Dover edition, first published in 1997, is a lightly edited but otherwise unabridged republication of music from "Serie I. Symphonien" (1900) of *Werke von Hector Berlioz,* originally published by Breitkopf & Härtel, Leipzig, 1900–1910.   Lists of instrumentation and performance notes are newly added.

International Standard Book Number: 0-486-29890-6

Manufactured in the United States of America
Dover Publications, Inc., 31 East 2nd Street, Mineola, N.Y. 11501

CONTENTS

Symphonie Fantastique
(Episode in the Life of an Artist)

Op. 14 (1830)

PROGRAMME

A young musician of unhealthily sensitive nature and endowed with vivid imagination has poisoned himself with opium in a paroxysm of lovesick despair. The narcotic dose he had taken was too weak to cause death but it has thrown him into a long sleep accompanied by the most extraordinary visions. In this condition his sensations, feelings and memories find utterance in his sick brain in the form of musical imagery. Even the beloved one takes the form of melody in his mind, like a fixed idea that is ever-returning, that he hears everywhere.

I. Visions. Passions.

At first the young musician thinks of the uneasy and nervous condition of his mind, of somber longings, of depression and joyous elation without recognizable cause—all that he had experienced before the beloved one appeared to him. Then he remembers the ardent love with which she suddenly inspired him; he thinks of his almost insane anxiety of mind, and his raging jealousy, of his reawakening love, of his religious consolation.

II. A ball

In a ballroom, amidst the confusion of a brilliant festival, he finds the loved one again.

III. In the countryside

It is a summer evening. He is in the countryside musing when he hears two young shepherds playing the *ranz des vaches* in alternation. This is the tune used by the Swiss to call their flocks together. This shepherd-duet, the surroundings, the soft whisperings of trees stirred by the zephyrs, some prospects of hope recently made known to him—all these sensations unite to impart a long-unknown repose to his heart and to lend a smiling color to his imagination.

And then she appears once more.

His heart stops beating . . . painful forebodings fill his soul. "Should she prove false to him!"

One of the shepherds resumes the melody, but the other answers him no more . . .

Sunset . . . distant rolling of thunder . . . loneliness . . . silence.

IV. The procession to the scaffold

He dreams that he had murdered his beloved, that he has been condemned to death and is being led to the scaffold. A march that is alternately somber and wild, brilliant and solemn, accompanies the procession . . . Tumultuous outbursts are followed without modulation by measured steps.

At last the "fixed idea" returns, for a moment a last thought of love is revived—then all is cut short by the death-blow.

V. Dream of a witches' sabbath

He dreams that he is present at a witches' dance, surrounded by horrible spirits, amidst sorcerers and monsters in many fearful forms, who have come to attend his funeral. Strange sounds, groans, shrill laughter, distant yells that other cries seem to answer.

The beloved melody is heard again but has its noble and shy character no longer; it has become a vulgar, trivial and grotesque kind of dance. *She* it is who comes to attend the witches' meeting. Friendly howls and shouts greet her arrival . . . She joins the infernal orgy . . . bells toll for the dead . . . a burlesque parody of the *Dies irae* . . . the witches' round-dance . . . the dance and the *Dies irae* are heard at the same time.

INSTRUMENTATION

2 Flutes [Flauti, Fl.]
Flute II doubles Piccolo [Flauto piccolo, Fl. picc.]

2 Oboes [Oboi, Ob.]
Oboe II doubles English Horn [Corno inglese, C.ingl.]
(Oboe I plays "behind the scene" in Movement III)

2 Clarinets in C, A, B♭ [Clarinetti, Clar. (Ut, La, Si♭)]

4 Horns in C, E♭, E, F, B♭-basso
[Corni, Cor. (Ut, Mi♭, Mi, Fa, Si♭ grave)]

4 Bassoons [Fagotti, Fag.]

2 Cornets in A, B♭ [Cornetti, C^tti (Cornets à pistons)
(La, Si♭)]

2 Trumpets in C, B♭ [Trombe, Tr. (Ut, Si♭)]

3 Trombones [Trombone/i, Tromb.]

2 Tubas [Tuba/e]

2 Harps [Arpa]

Timpani [Timpani, Timp.]
4 players required in Movement III

Percussion
Snare Drum [Tamburo, Tamb.]
Cymbals [Cinelli]
Bass Drum [Gran Tamburo, Gr. Tamb. (Grosse Caisse)]
2 Bells in C, G [Campane, Camp. (Glocken) (Ut, Sol)]
(Bells play "behind the scene" in Movement V)

Violins I, II [Violino, Viol.]
Violas [Viola/e]
Cellos [Violoncello, Vc(e)llo/i]
Basses [Contrabasso, C.B.]

PERFORMANCE NOTES

[The original large-size edition of this work incorporates editorial score notes and footnotes that are paraphrased below for easy reference. They are keyed by page and measure numbers. A few minor remarks have been deleted.]

Mvmt. I

p. 7, m. 64: One bar of this tempo equals a quarter note of the preceding section.

p. 32, m. 509: The whole orchestra plays as softly as possible.

Mvmt. II

Instrumentation: Berlioz later added the part for *Cornetto in A* to the autograph. The original editors recommended its omission, notating the part in small notes.

p. 35, m. 43 / Vln. I: The diagonal line between notes indicates a *portamento*.

Mvmt. III

p. 58-9 / Oboe I: Oboe plays behind the scenes in mm. 3–20, then reenters the orchestra.

p. 58 / The four timpanists: In the last movement (finale), percussionists 3 and 4 play the bass drum; percussionist 2 plays the second pair of timpani.

Mvmt. IV

p. 74 / Composer's note: "In this movement, the winds may be doubled."

p. 74 / Timpani: The first 8th of each sextuplet is struck two-handed, with both sticks. The remaining five 8ths are played with the right-hand stick alone.

p. 88, m. 123 / Timpani: The composer's indication "senza sordini" suggests that Berlioz wanted the timpani muffled at the beginning of this piece.

p. 92, mm. 154-5 / Composer's note: "The progression from the D-flat triad [m. 154] to the G minor triad [m. 155] is correct. The composer requests the violinists and violists not to 'correct' their parts by placing a flat before the D of the G minor chord."

Mvmt. V

p. 95 / Bass Drum: The bass drum is to be placed upright [its head parallel to the floor] and treated as a drum; players 3 and 4 play it with sponge-headed beaters.

p. 106, m. 102 / Bells: Available bells should be capable of intoning C's and G's in at least one of the octaves [registers] shown in the score. Otherwise, the parts should be played on the piano, with the doublings performed as written.

SYMPHONIE FANTASTIQUE, OP. 14

I.

Rêveries. Passions. • *Visions. Passions.*

Allegro agitato e appassionato assai. (♩ = 132.)

Une mesure de ce mouvement équivaut au quart de la précédente.
Ein Takt dieses Zeitmaasses wie ein Viertel des vorhergehenden.
One bar of this time-measure is equal to a quarter-bar of the preceding movement.

Allegro agitato e appassionato assai. (♩ = 132.)

17
400
Fl. I.
Flauto piccolo.
Ob.
a 2.
Clar.
cresc. molto
Cor.
III.
Fag.
cresc. molto
Ctti
I.
cresc. molto
a 2.
Tr.
Timp.
cresc. molto
Viol. I. div.
cresc. molto
cresc. molto
Viol. II. div.
cresc. molto
Viola.
cresc. molto
cresc. molto
Vcelli. div.
cresc. molto
C. B.
cresc. molto
17

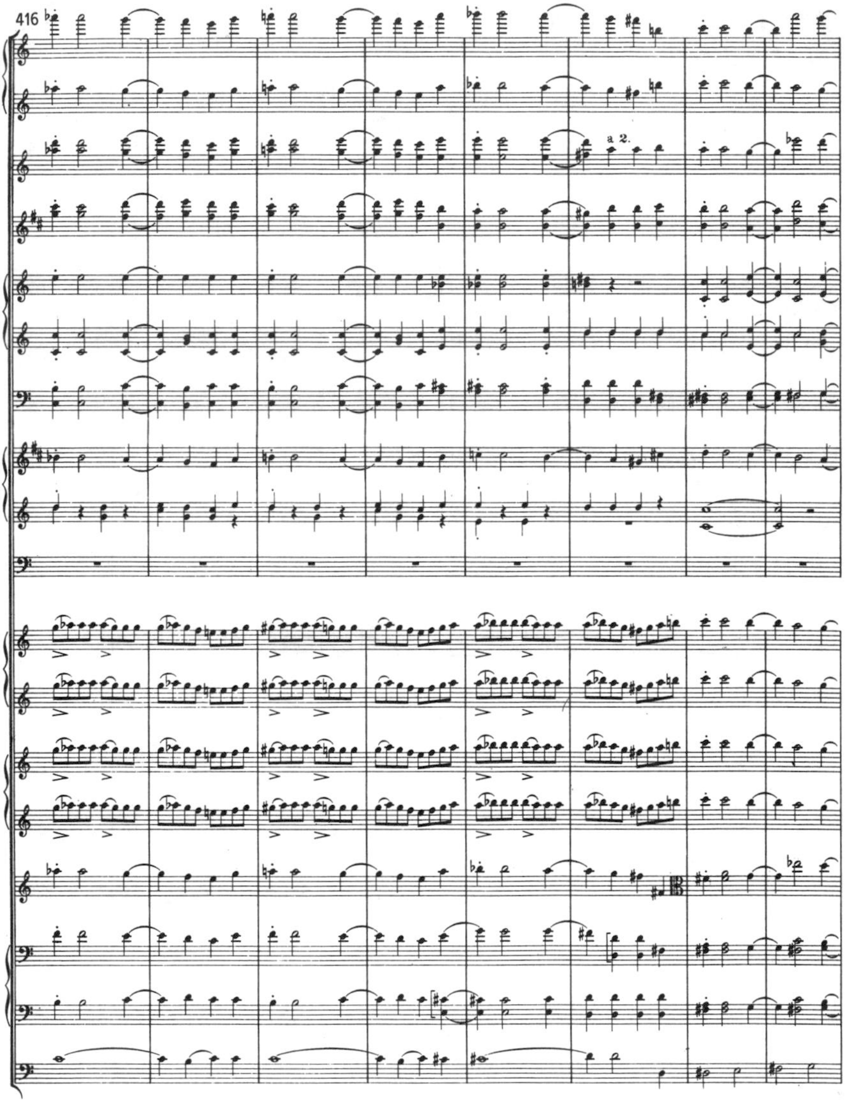
416
a 2.

459
Tempo I. più animato.
Fl.
I.
mf
cresc.
Fl. picc.
Ob.
a 2
Clar.
Fag.
a 2.
Timp.
Viol. I.
Viol. II. div.
pizz.
Tempo I. più animato.
470
20
Cor.
Tr.
Timp.
ff
sf
unis.
div.
arco
20

II.

Un bal • *A ball*

109
Fl.
Ob.
Clar.
Cor.
Ctto
Viol.
Vcllo.
C.B.
26
quasi niente
poco f
119
I.
p espressivo
128
Vcllo. e C.B.

185
Fl.
Ob.
Clar.
Cor. I. II.
Ctto
Arpa II.
Viol.
sf
191
Fl.
p cresc.
f
Ob.
Clar.
Cor. I. II.
Ctto
Arpa I.
poco f
(p)
Arpa II.
Viol.
Vcllo. I.
pizz.
Vcllo. II.
C. B.
cresc.

199
Fl.
Ob.
Clar.
Cor. I. II.
Cttⁿ
Arpa I
Arpa II.
Viol.
Vcllo.
C. B.
arco
29
207
30
I.
pizz.
arco
div.
dimin.
poco f

216
Fl.
Ob.
cresc. poco
a poco
cresc. molto
Clar.
Cor. I. II.
Arpa II.
Viol.
arco
poco f
cresc.
pizz.
224
Flauto piccolo.
C^tto
Arpa I.
G. P.

III.

Scène aux champs • *In the countryside*

58

52
Fl.
Ob.
Clar.
Cor. I. II.
Fag.
Viol.
cresc.
sf
p
f
arco
pizz.
59
Fl.
Ob. I. II
Clar.
Cor. IV. (in C)
Fag.
a 2.
Viol.
unis.
mf
f dim.
39

103
42
poco animato
Fl.
Ob.
Clar.
Cor. I. II in F.
Cor. III in Es.
Cor. IV in C.
Fag.
Timp. I.
Viol.
cresc.
f cresc.
Baguettes de bois.
Holzschlägel.
Wooden drum-sticks.
ff
a 2.
42 poco animato
109
rallent.
dim.
p morendo
pp
Tempo I.
p
pizz.
tr.
Cor. I. II.
Cor. III.
Cor. IV.
Tempo I.

IV.

Marche au supplice • *Procession to the scaffold*

74

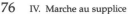

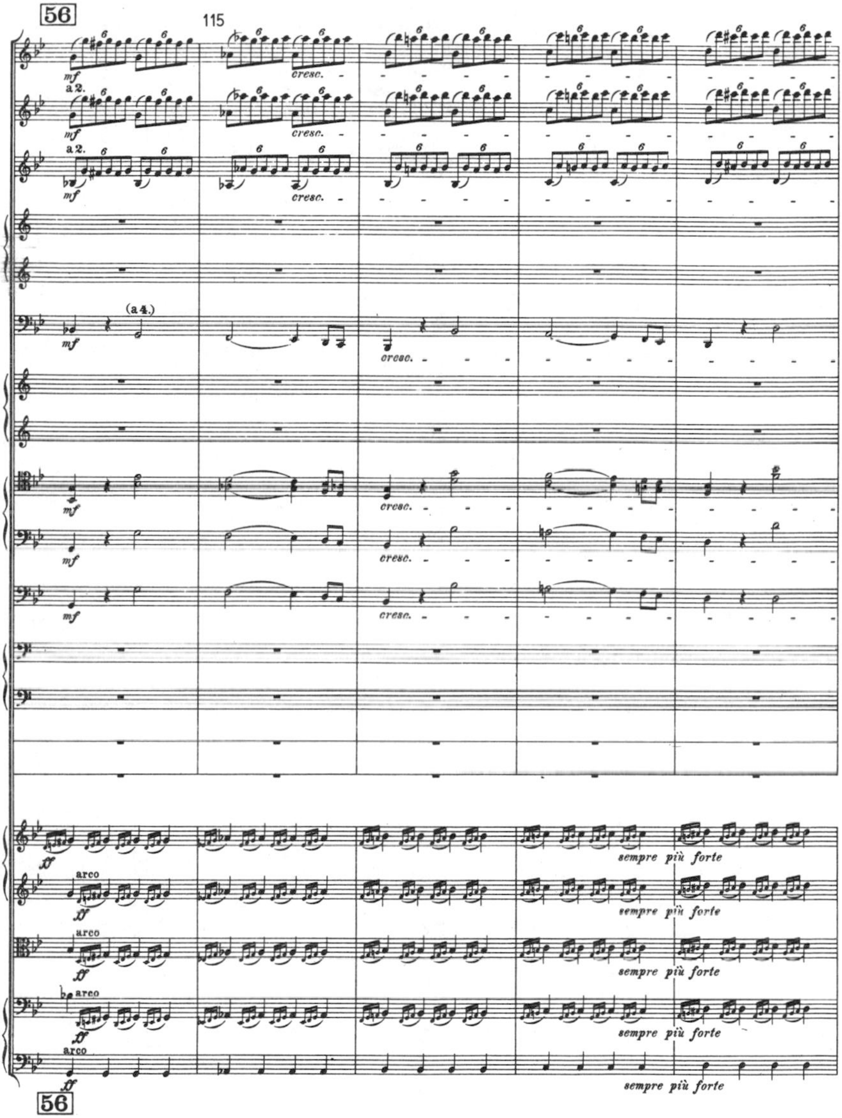
56
115
mf
a 2.
cresc.
(a 4.)
arco
ff
sempre più forte
56

136

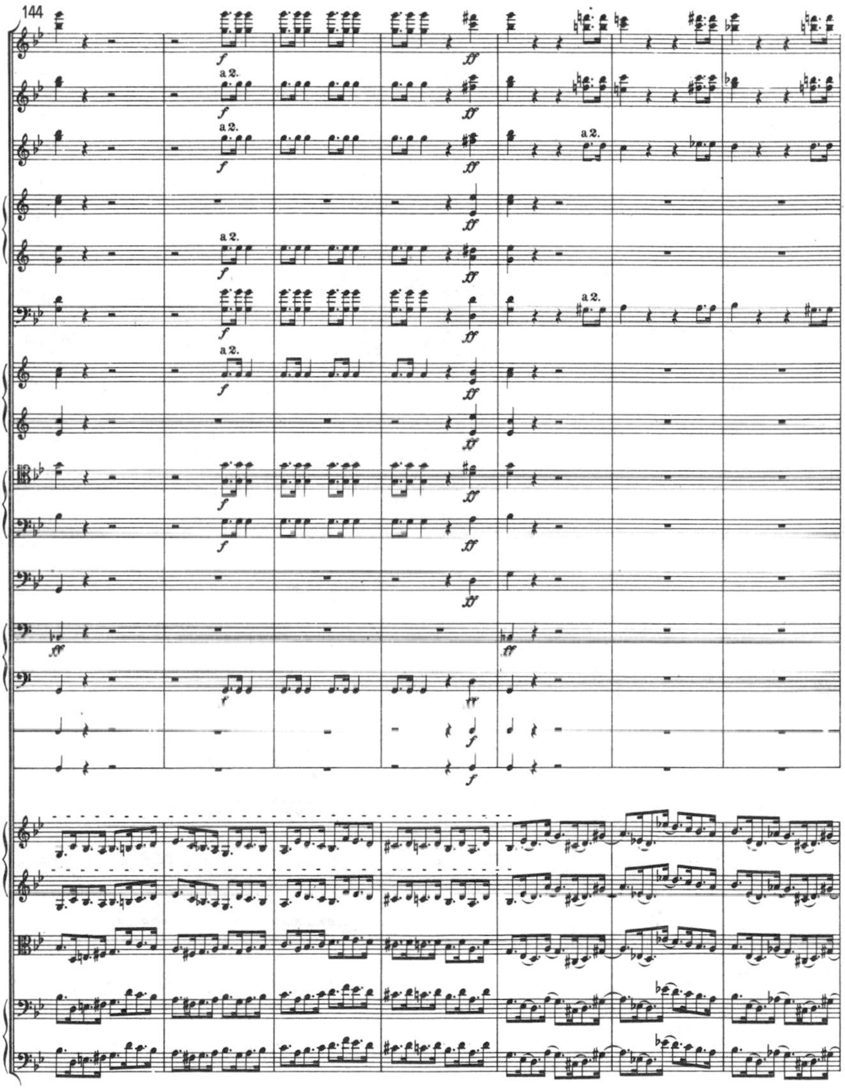
144
a 2.
f
ff

V.

Songe d'une nuit du Sabbat • *Dream of a witches' sabbath*

13

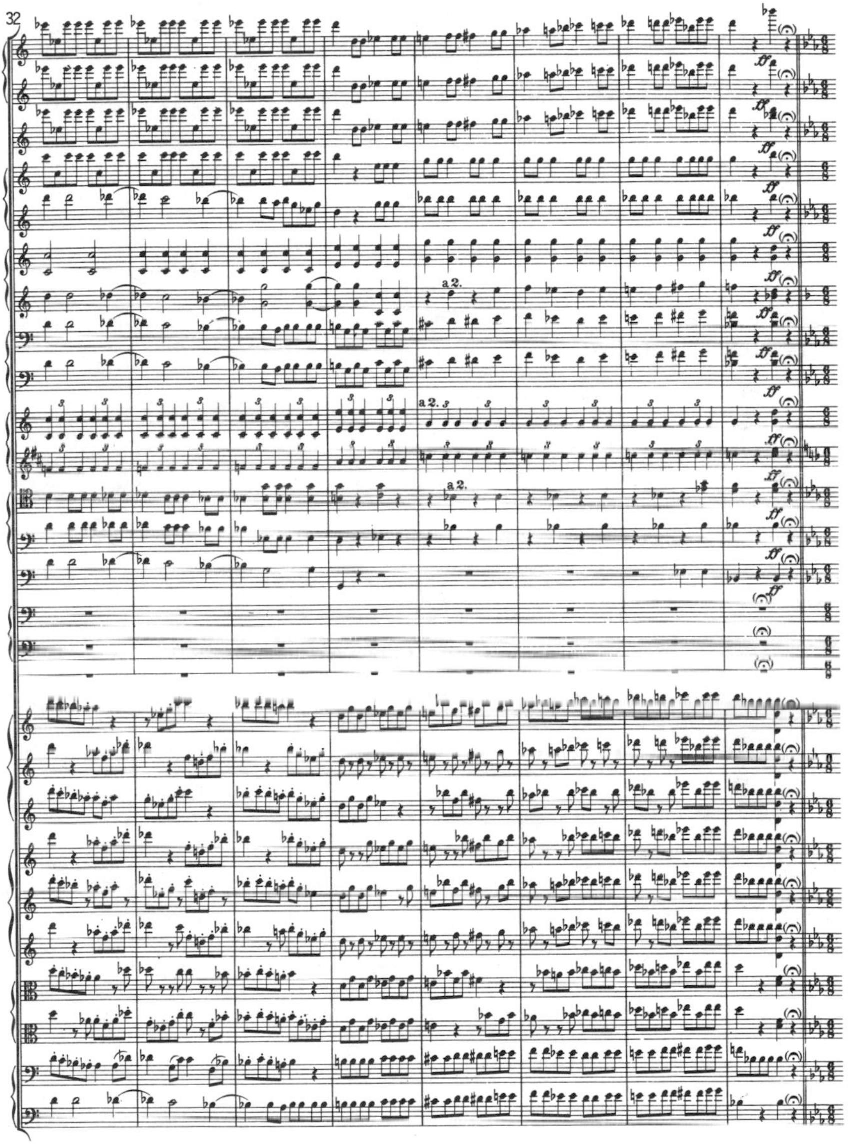
32
a 2.
a 2.
a 2.

67
Fl. I.
Fl. picc.
Ob.
Clar.
Cor.
Fag.
a 4.
Tr.
Ctti
Tromb.
Tuba I.
Timp.
Viol.
a 2.
ff

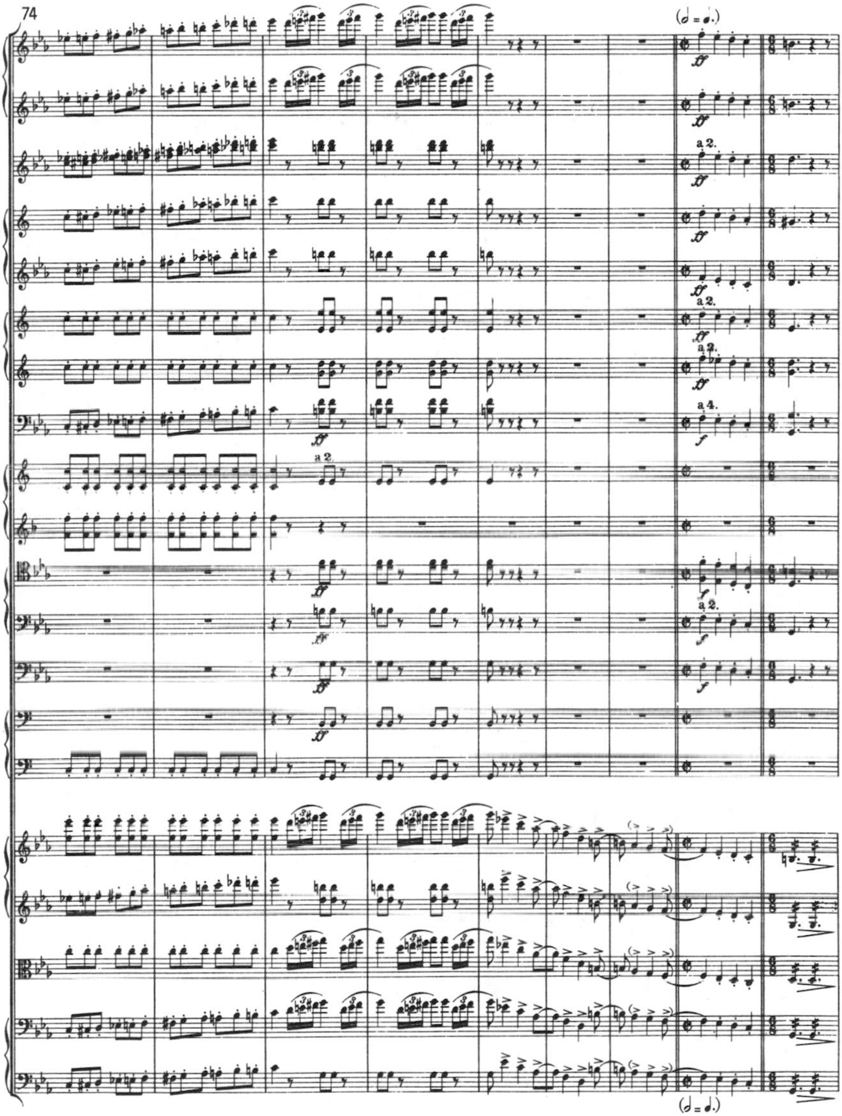
74
a 2.
a 4.
ff
f

171

196

221 **69**

69

Ronde du Sabbat.
Witches' round dance.
Poco meno mosso.*⁾

245

Poco meno mosso.

*⁾ Le mouvement,qui a dû s'animer un peu, redevient ici comme au chiffre ⑥③ Allegro (♩.= 104)
Das Zeitmaass,welches sich etwas belebt hat, wird hier wieder wie bei Ziffer ⑥③ Allegro (♩.= 104)
The movement, which has animated itself, is here again as at number ⑥③ Allegro (♩.= 104)

272

289

306

313

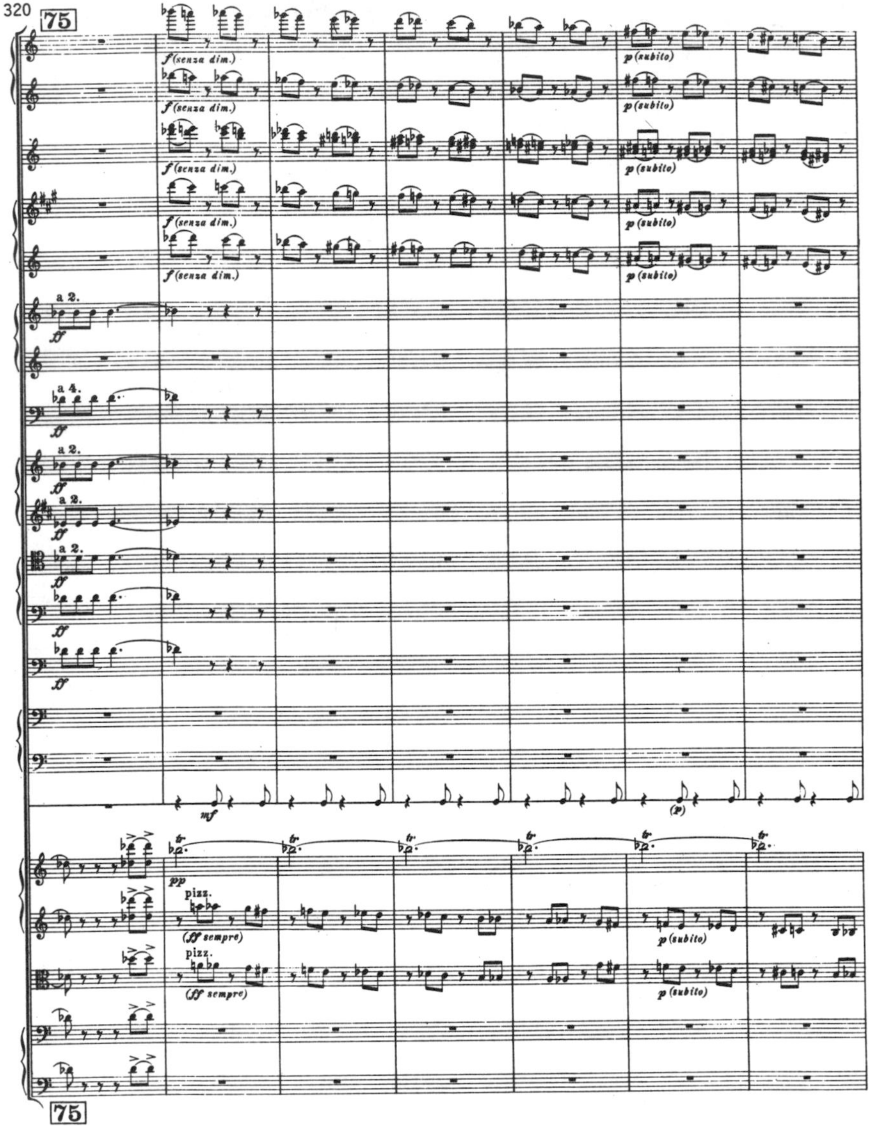
320
75
f (senza dim.)
p (subito)
a 2.
a 4.
ff
mf
(p)
tr
pp
pizz.
(ff sempre)
75

335

80
389
(cresc. molto)
ff
mf (cresc. molto)
f
a 4.
a 2.
cresc. molto
div.
unis.
80

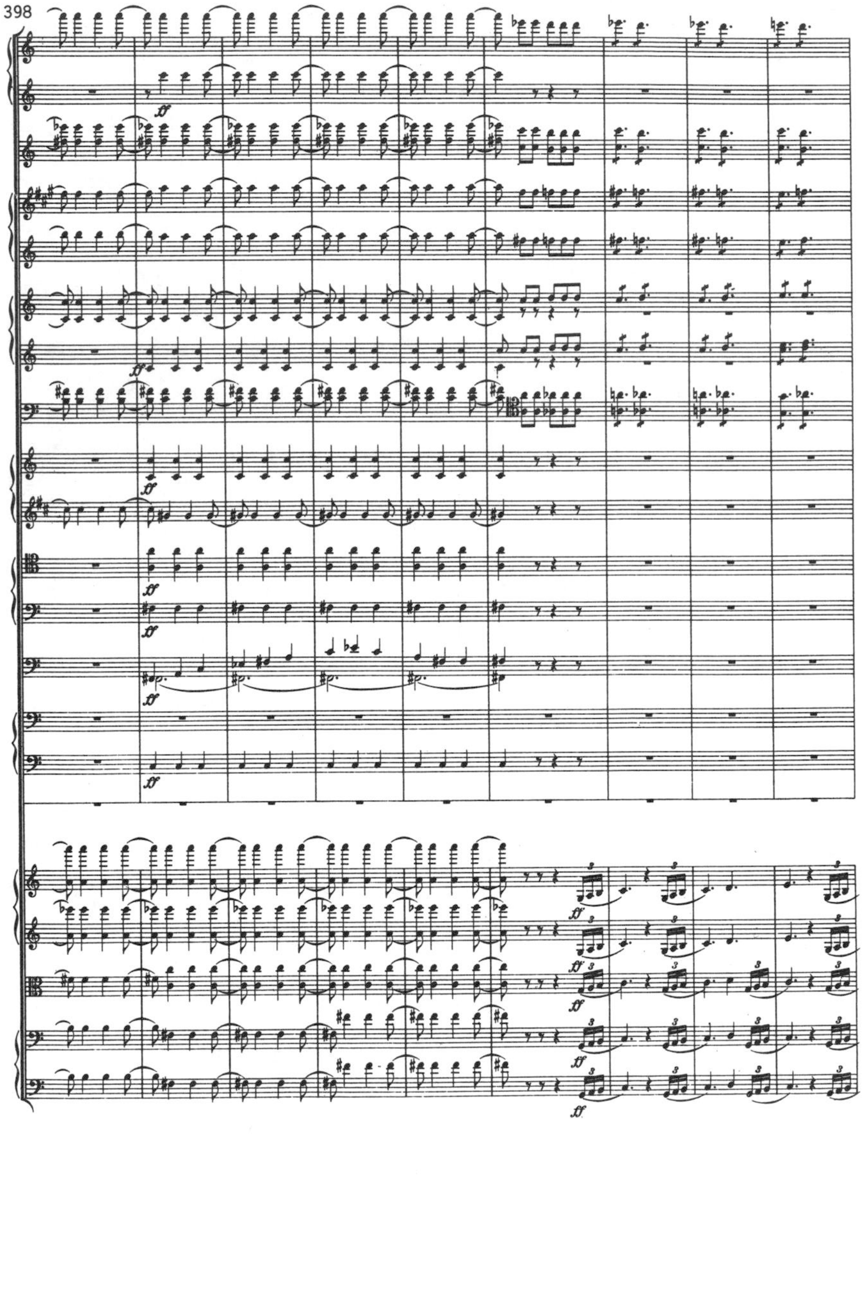
398
ff

414   Dies irae et Ronde du Sabbat (ensemble).
Dies irae and witches' round dance (together).

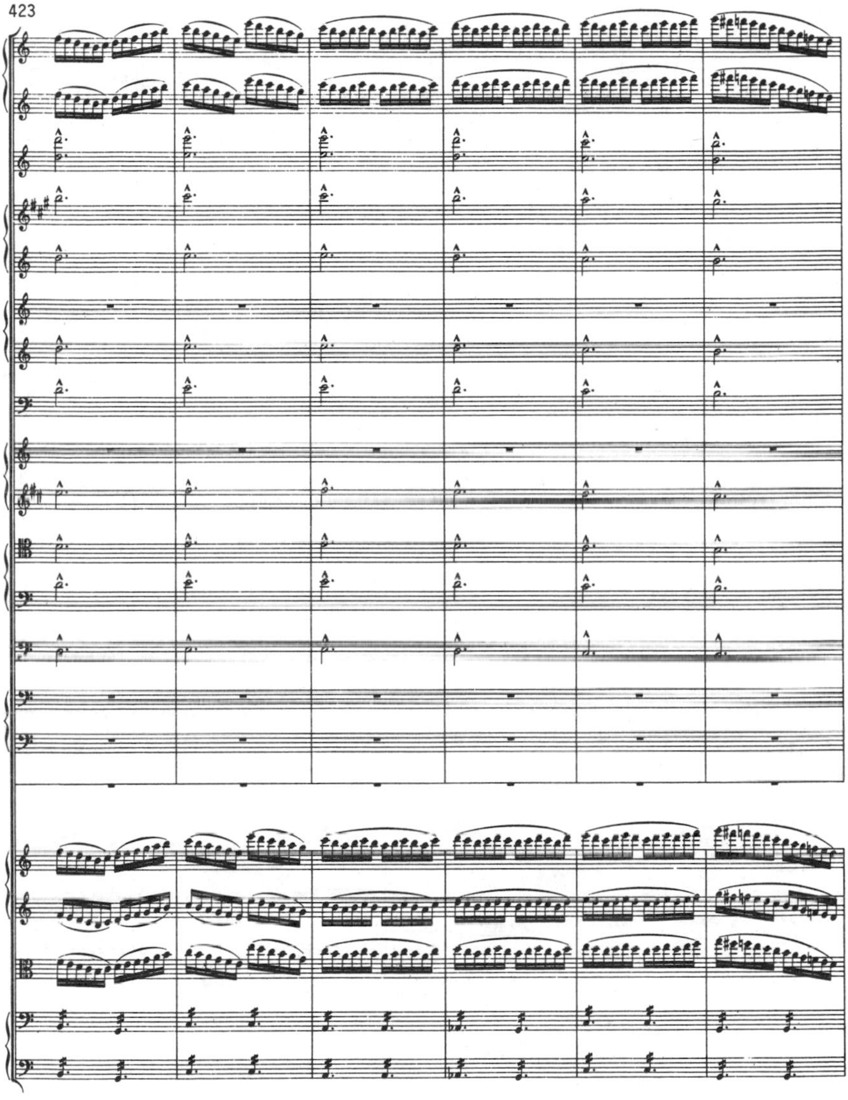
423

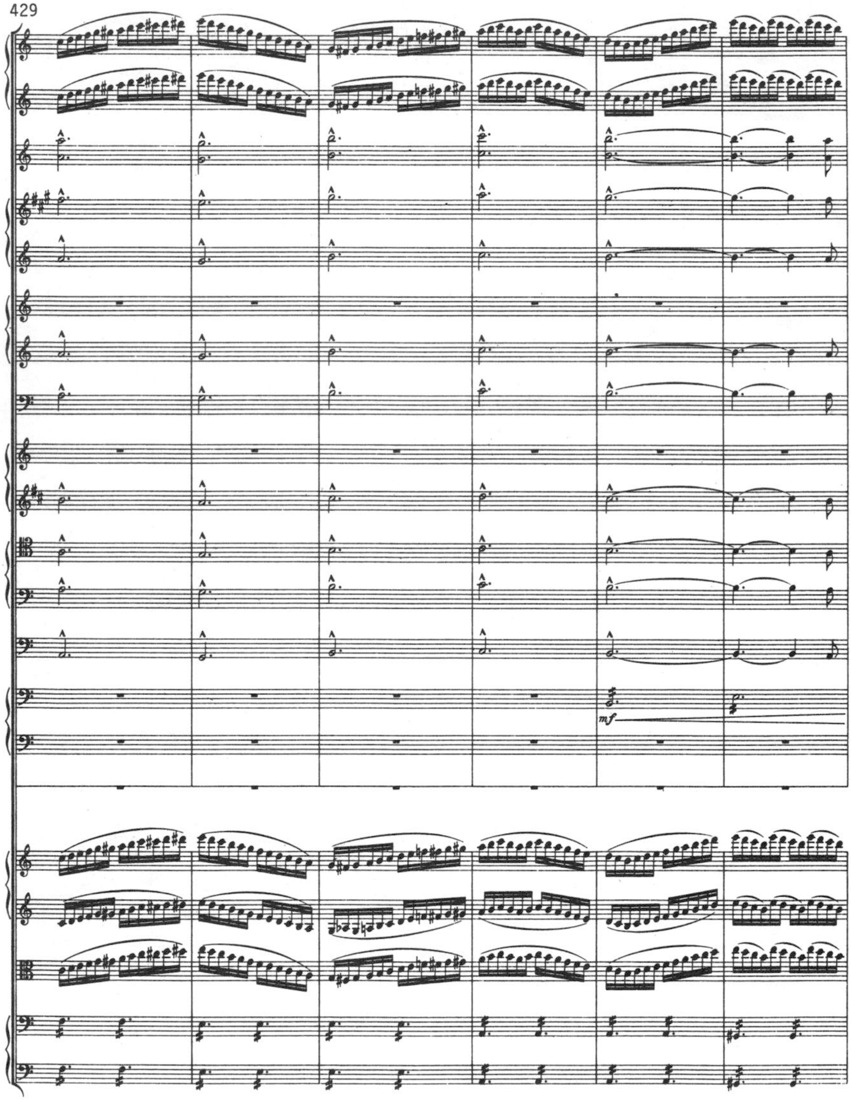
429
mf

448

474

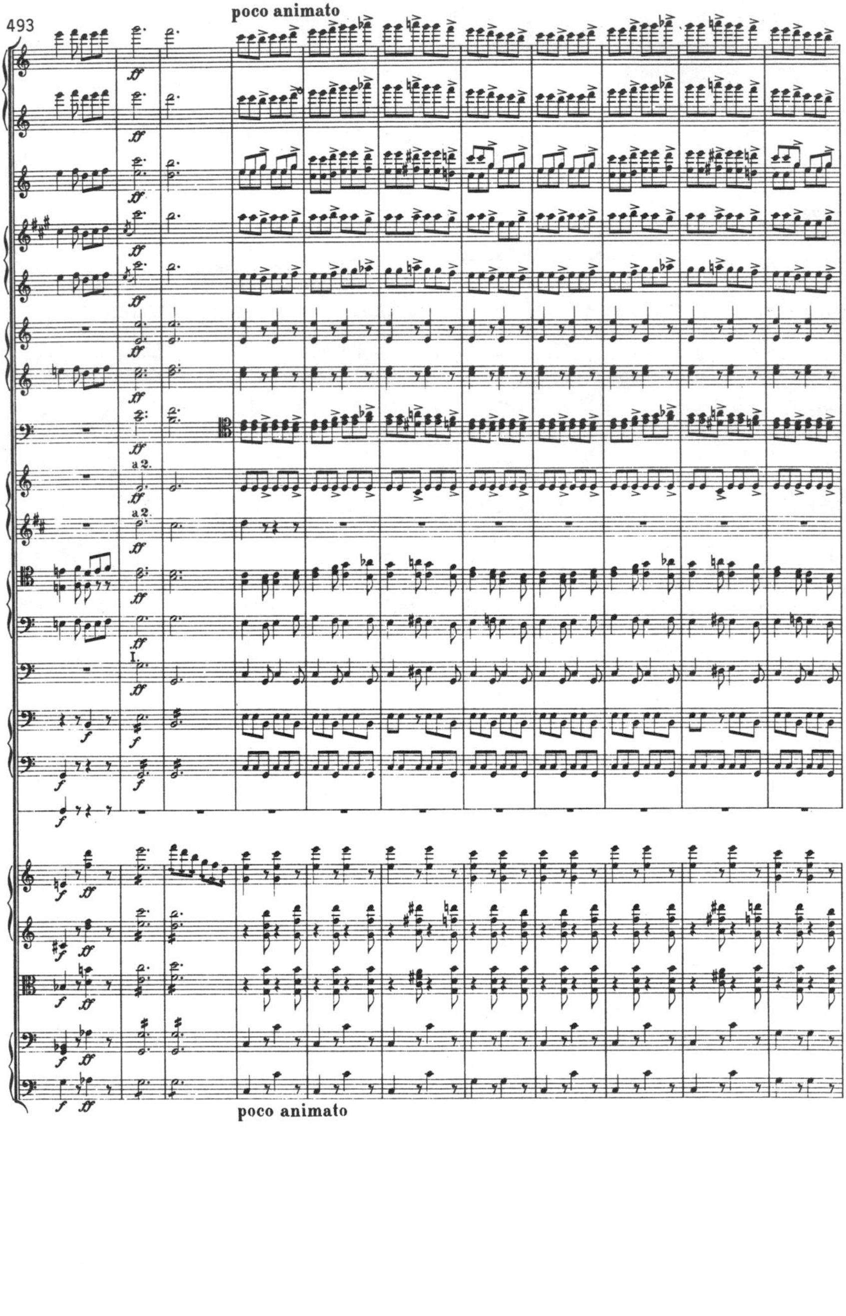
poco animato
493
a 2.
a 2.
I.
poco animato

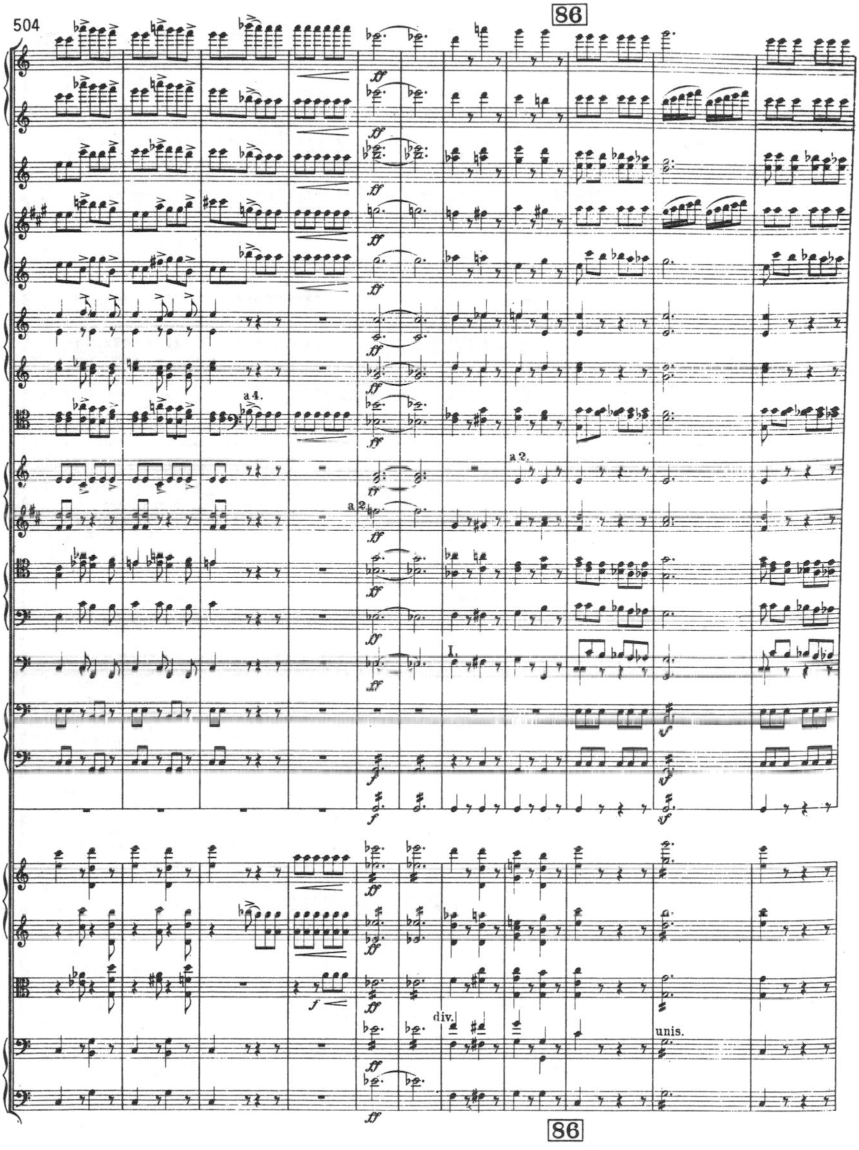

86
504
a 4.
a 2.
a2
I.
div.
unis.
86

Coup frappé sur une Cymbale avec une baguette
couverte d'éponge ou un tampon.
Schlag auf ein Becken mit einem Schwamm-
schlägel oder Klöppel.
Struck on a cymbal with a sponge-headed
drum-stick.

Cinelli.

END OF EDITION